THE LONG RED ROAD

Brett C Leonard

BROADWAY PLAY PUBLISHING INC
New York
www.broadwayplaypublishing.com
info@broadwayplaypublishing.com

THE LONG RED ROAD
© Copyright 2010 Brett C Leonard

Image design by Kelly Rickert
First printing: December 2010
I S B N: 978-0-88145-464-2
Book design: Marie Donovan
Typographic controls & page make-up: Adobe InDesign
Typeface: Palatino
Printed and bound in the U S A

THE LONG RED ROAD was first produced at the Goodman Theater (Robert Falls, Artistic Director) in Chicago, opening on 13 February 2010. The cast and creative contributors were:

SAM .... Tom Hardy
ANNIE .... Greta Honold
BOB .... Chris McGarry
SANDRA .... Katy Sullivan
TASHA .... Fiona Robert
CLIFTON .... Markos Akiaten

Director .... Philip Seymour Hoffman
Assistant director .... Scott Illingworth
Scenic design .... Eugene Lee
Lighting design .... Edward Pierce
Costumes .... Janice Pytel
Original music & sound .... Ray Nardelli &
Joshua Horvath
Stage manager .... Kimberly Osgood

CHARACTERS & SETTING

SAMMY, *white, 32*
ANNIE, *white, early 20s*
BOB, *white, 36*
TASHA, *white, 13*
SANDRA, *white, 30s*
CLIFTON, *Native American, Lakota, 50s*

South Dakota and Kansas. The Present.

for my brother Bruce

dedicated to the memory of Marcos Akiaten

ACT ONE

Scene 1

(Studio apartment)

(South Dakota)

(Cheaply furnished, small, old. A double bed. A bedside lamp with a torn shade glows its yellow 60 watt bulb. Cigarettes fill an ashtray. A few booze bottles are strewn about.)

(A chest of drawers in a corner. On top is a ten-year-old 19" television with an antenna. There is a small round wooden table with two mismatched chairs.)

(A small kitchen area is adjacent—cheap linoleum floor, a fridge, stove, toaster.)

(A door leads to a small bathroom off stage.)

(On one wall is a cheaply framed painting of a Native American Man, a Lakota Indian Chief, in face paint and head dress. Nailed to another wall is a replica buffalo skin. On the floor is a fake bearskin rug.)

(Also on the floor are SAMMY, *white, 32, and* ANNIE, *white, early 20's. Wrapped in a Lakota blanket)*

(They're fucking. Making love. Trying to connect. ANNIE *is on top.)*

SAMMY: I love you, I love you. Tell me you hate me.

ANNIE: I hate you.

SAMMY: Tell me again.

ANNIE: I hate you…

SAMMY: …I love you…

ANNIE: …I hate you. I hate your guts.

SAMMY: Tell me you hate my guts an' I'm a piece a' shit.

ANNIE: You're a filthy piece of shit and I hate you.

SAMMY: I'm a low-life.

ANNIE: You're a disaster.

SAMMY: I love you.

ANNIE: I hate you.

SAMMY: Tell me I ain't shit an' don't deserve you.

ANNIE: You don't deserve me.

SAMMY: I'm a fuckin' drunk.

ANNIE: You're a loser and an asshole—don't stop, right there, don't stop.

SAMMY: I deserve nothing!

ANNIE: Fuck you!

SAMMY: I'm a scumfuck fuckbag…

ANNIE: …You're a piece a' garbage, oh yeah, yeah, don't stop, don't…

SAMMY: …Yeah…

ANNIE: …Yes yes!…

SAMMY: …I love you…

ANNIE: …I hate you…

SAMMY: …I love you so much…

ANNIE: …I hate you MORE—YES, YES!…

SAMMY: …Yes…

ANNIE: …You're a drunk, you're a murderer…

SAMMY: ...You're beautiful, you're perfect...

ANNIE: ...Don't stop, don't stop...

SAMMY: ...Oh God, you're so perfect—I'm gonna cum...

ANNIE: ...No!...

SAMMY: ...Baby, I'm, I can't, I, I...

ANNIE: ...No, no!!...

SAMMY: ...Uuaagghh, I'm *tryin' not to*...

ANNIE: ...no-no-no-no-no-no-no- don't stop, don't st... no, *don't stop!*...

SAMMY: ...Shit, fuck, I'm cumming, I'm cummin—g...

ANNIE: ...Fuck fuck fuck fuck fuck fuck fuck...

SAMMY: ...Oh God, oh God!!!...

ANNIE: ...Yeah baby, yeah baby, yeah baby...

SAMMY: ...don't leave, don't leave me...please...

ANNIE: ...Sshh—sshh... I'm right here.

SAMMY: Don't leave...don't...oh, fuck...

ANNIE: I love you.

SAMMY: Don't go...

ANNIE: ...I won't...

SAMMY: ...I love you...

ANNIE: ...I'm right here...

SAMMY: ...Don't go... Don't leave...

ANNIE: ...Sshh...sshh... I love you too... I'm right here, Sam... I'm right here.

Scene 2

(A mushroom barn.)

(Kansas)

(Rows and rows of Grow Bags hang from the ceiling. Mushrooms grow through holes, forming clusters. Shitake mushrooms. And Oyster mushrooms—yellow, pink, blue, gray, brown. Other items include a pressure cooker, jars, lids, pots, pans, alcohol lamp, small scale, large scale, petri dishes, boxes, rope, tool box, trash bags, test tubes, a fan, an automatic misting system, and gauges that read humidity and temperature. Rows of other species of mushroom grow on long greenhouse tables and inside plaster pots.)

(Sitting on a stool, tending to the mushrooms, is BOB MCHENRY, *white, 36. Standing to the side, by the door, is* TASHA, *white, 13.)*

BOB: *(Without looking at her)* An' then I'll burn 'em, ya unnerstand? I burn 'em, they're no more. Rip 'em inta lil' pieces, throw 'em inta flames, leave nothin', no choice. Changes come... Parts come... Things grow, ya unnerstand? They change. *(Beat)* Polyporus Tuberaster. Stone Mushroom. It blooms and...sprouts... ...like a beautiful velvet. Got a nice mild flavor to 'em too. Good for sauté. *(Beat)* Or these, the Maitake. Grifola Frondosa, "Hen a' the Woods". *(Beat)* Your mother prefers the Pearl...Pleurotus Ostreatus. They're okay. *(Beat)* We gotta have rules, Tosh. It's our fault we ain't been good enuf enforcin'. You're thirteen years old. Soon you'll be fourteen...fifteen. You're a little girl on the verge become a big one. You understand? *(Beat)* I asked you a question. Do you understand?

TASHA: Yeah.

BOB: Wassat?

TASHA: I said 'yeah'.

Bob: You're a lil' girl, Tosh. You're not a goddamn prostitute.

Scene 3

(Studio apartment)

(ANNIE is sitting up in bed, a pillow propped behind her back. The sheet and blanket are still on the floor. She stares without interest at the television's poor reception, airing a long-cancelled half-hour comedy.)

(From the offstage bathroom we hear SAMMY vomiting into the toilet. Again and again. Pause. And again. Pause. And again.)

(ANNIE gets off the bed. She carries a bottle of whiskey into the bathroom, offstage.)

(She re-enters. As the TV continues its re-run, and the vomiting slowly subsides, ANNIE picks the Lakota blanket off the floor and moves to the bed. She begins making the bed.)

(SAMMY enters from the bathroom, bottle in hand. He puts the bottle on the nightstand, on his side of the bed. He says nothing. She says nothing.)

(He helps her finish making the bed.)

(He carries the bottle to the small, round table. He sits. He lights a cigarette.)

(ANNIE gets on the bed. She looks at the TV, again without interest.)

(Pause)

(SAMMY drinks straight from the bottle.)

(Pause)

ANNIE: You wanna watch TV?

(SAMMY shrugs.)

(Pause)

(With the remote, ANNIE turns off the T V.)

(Pause)

ANNIE: You wanna come to sleep?

SAMMY: *(Meaning "no, I'm not tired")* I'm alright.

(Pause)

ANNIE: Try to sleep in the bed tonight, Sam. *(Beat)* I want you to.

(SAMMY drinks. ANNIE turns off the bedside lamp. She lies down, tries to sleep.)

(Long pause)

SAMMY: You seen that thing on the T V 'bout today with them tourists? Mmph? What happened at the K O A, 'round Rushmore? Mmph? You seen it? Annabelle?

ANNIE: *(Meaning "no")* Mmm-mm.

SAMMY: Outside Rushmore, 'bout thirty-forty minutes. Might be you could catch it if ya turn it back on. They was showin' it earlier, least. *(Beat)* Annie? *(Beat)* Annie, you heard? *(Pause)* Guy got mauled ta death on his family vacation. By a black bear in brown coat. News morons callin' grizzly. Brother-in-law gets the whole thing on videotape. *(Beat)* Ya turn it on ya might still see it—minus any gore or graphics or anything. They blurred out the details when I saw. Too much for the uh…too much for the average person, I s'pose…the viewer. Rather see the weather. They favorite sports team. No blood an' guts. No big ol' teeth marks. Chunks a' flesh torn. Missin' limbs. No truth. *(Beat)* His brother-in-law stood by pointin' a camera. *(Beat)* Mmph? *(Beat)* Annie? *(Beat)* You like that? *(Beat)* They got five kids with 'em…two wives…only thing put ta use… the camera. *(Beat)* Peaceful getaway. *(Beat)*

Don't know 'nuf ta tie his food up a tree. *(He rubs his chest with his fist. He drinks. Pause. He drinks. He rubs his chest.)* Annie? *(Beat)* Babe? *(Beat)* It's happenin'. *(Beat)* Annabelle? *(Beat)* Baby? *(He drinks. Pause)* Hey? *(Beat)* Hey? *(Long pause. Softly)* G'nite. *(He drinks.)*

Scene 4

(A bedroom and adjacent bathroom)

(BOB and SANDRA, white, 30s, get ready for bed.))

(She walks with a limp.)

(She brushes her teeth with an electric toothbrush. He uses a traditional toothbrush.)

(She washes her face. He washes his filthy hands. He gargles with hydrogen peroxide and water.)

(She flushes the toilet.)

(He moves to the bed.)

(She puts cream under her eyes.)

(He gets under the covers.)

(She enters the bedroom.)

(She sits on her side of the bed. She removes two low-quality prosthetics. Each leg is cut off near the knee.)

(She gets under the covers.)

(They lie on their backs, two-three feet of empty space between them.)

BOB: I talked to 'r. *(Beat)* I said I talked to 'r. *(Beat)* I told 'r she come home or go out, wherever…clothes we ain't like, ain't bought…she borrowed, found 'em, stole 'em… I'll rip 'em up an' burn 'em. I told 'r she's thirteen years old. I told 'r she ain't no prostitute.

SANDRA: Her friends are the same.

BOB: I ain't have no responsibility for no friends.

(Pause)

SANDRA: You called her a prostitute?

BOB: I said she was *not* a prostitute. I told'r she's a young girl.

(Beat)

SANDRA: Wha'd she say?

BOB: Said "momma's right…you can be a real asshole." Then she run off. *(Pause)* I'm gonna try ta sleep now. *(Beat)* 'Less ya wanna stay up some? *(Beat)* Together, I mean, you know…for a lil' while?

(Long pause)

BOB: G'nite. *(He turns off his bedside lamp.)*

SANDRA: Goodnight.

(Pause)

(SANDRA turns off her bedside lamp. They lie on their sides, their backs two-three feet apart.)

(Pause)

SANDRA: I don't always think you're a asshole. I'm sorry I told 'r that.

(Beat)

BOB: I don't always think you're a asshole neither. *(Pause)* G'nite.

SANDRA: G'nite.

Scene 5

(Studio apartment)

(Morning)

(Sun fights through slivers in the blinds. It beats down on SAMMY, *sound asleep/passed-out on the floor.)*

(On the table, next to empty bottles, almost empty bottles, and an overflowing ashtray, there's a pen and a 5" x 8" spiral notebook.)

*(*ANNIE *enters from the bathroom, ready for work.)*

(She moves to the table. She picks up the notebook and rips out two pages on which SAMMY *has written. She leaves the notebook on the table.)*

(She goes to her side of the bed, reaches under the bed and takes out a shoebox, places it on the bed. She puts the two pages she ripped out of the notebook into the shoebox. She puts the shoebox back under the bed.)

(She goes to SAMMY. *She gently nudges him with her foot. No response. She nudges again. Again. Her gentleness grows a bit more aggressive, but doesn't become extreme or violent.)*

ANNIE: Sammy. Sammy, get up. Get up, Sam. Come on, wake up.

*(*SAMMY *stirs awake, barely, and is disoriented.)*

ANNIE: Go to the bed, Sam, go on… Try to. *(She leans down and kisses his forehead.)* Have a good day.

*(*ANNIE *moves to the front door. She stops and looks back.* SAMMY *is slowly moving, trying to get to his knees.)*

ANNIE: I love you. *(Beat)* I love you.

*(*SAMMY *half-nods in an attempt at reciprocation:)*

SAMMY: Me too. *(He reaches for the cigarettes on the table. His hand shakes.)*

ANNIE: Remember to eat. *(Beat)* Sam? *(Beat)* Eat
something.

*(SAMMY lights a cigarette. He coughs. He rubs his chest
with his fist.)*

(ANNIE exits.)

*(SAMMY looks around. He reaches for a chair. His shakes
continue. With difficulty, he manages to sit in the chair. He
smokes. He gets his hand on a bottle of whiskey. He clutches
it, but doesn't lift it. With the help of his other hand he
moves the bottle to his lips. He drinks. He drinks again. He
drinks again.)*

*(His shakes begin to subside. He breathes more deeply, more
relaxed. He smokes. He drinks. He drinks again.)*

*(He looks at the notebook and pen. He picks up the notebook
and leafs through a few blank pages. He carries the notebook
and pen to the chest of drawers. He puts it on top of the
dresser.)*

*(He lifts an empty, green, canvas duffle bag off the floor.
He puts it on the kitchen counter. He opens a cabinet and
removes pots and pans.)*

*(He puts the pots and pans into the duffle bag. He zips the
bag closed.)*

*(He carries the bag into the main room of the studio. He
hangs it on two metal hooks drilled into the ceiling.)*

*(He hits the bag with his bare fists. One punch at a time.
Slowly, in no rush. Punch. Punch. Punch. Then a bit
harder…Punch. Punch. And harder… Punch-punch-
punch… He exhausts himself. He stops punching.)*

Scene 6

(The bedroom)

(Morning)

(BOB is gently kissing SANDRA's sleeping neck and cheek. She stirs, but doesn't wake. He continues, his hands begin to roam.)

(She moves farther away.)

(His hand makes its way under the sheets, down to her crotch.)

(She removes his hand.)

(He turns onto his side—his back to hers.)

(He sits up on his side of the bed.)

(Pause)

(He walks to the bathroom, turns on the shower, gets in.)

(She tries to get more sleep.)

(Silence...other than the sound of the shower.)

(TASHA enters. She looks at SANDRA, whose eyes are still closed.)

(She looks to the bathroom, at BOB in the shower. She stares.)

(Suddenly...)

SANDRA: Get outta here—go on, git out!

(The shower stops, TASHA continues looking toward BOB in the bathroom.)

SANDRA: I said git out, turn your eyes.

(TASHA looks at her mother. SANDRA remains in bed, sitting up.)

SANDRA: I said go, Tasha, git out. Now.

(BOB appears, standing in the bathroom doorway, wet, a towel around his waist.)

BOB: Everything okay? Tosh? Mmph? Sandy?

(SANDRA *and* TASHA *look at* BOB.)

BOB: I'm makin' eggs for breakfast. Bacon-mushroom, Pleurotus Ostreatus. Your mother's favorite. Why don'choo go on now. Go on, pour yourself a glass a' juice. We'll be soon enuf. Go on.

(TASHA *exits.*)

BOB: Tosh? Tasha?!

(TASHA *returns.*)

BOB: Shut the door, please. An' lock it.

(TASHA *locks the door and exits.*)

SANDRA: She was watchin' you in the shower.

BOB: We need ta remember ta lock the door. *(Beat)* I'm gonna make omelettes. *(Beat)* I gotta take a shit. *(He enters the bathroom.)*

Scene 7

(Studio apartment)

(SAMMY *is sitting on the foot of the bed…sweating… spent…sipping from a bottle.*)

(Silence)

(Lights remain on SAMMY *as they rise on:)*

(A run-down classroom.)

(ANNIE *teaches young, elementary schoolchildren on a Lakota Indian Reservation. She reads from* A People's History of the United States.)

ANNIE: Listen up, class. Quiet please. *(She holds up one finger, then a second, then a third. Pause. Reads)* "When Columbus and his sailors came ashore, carrying swords, the Arawak (natives) ran to greet them,

brought them food, water, gifts…" Columbus wrote
in his diary… "They brought us parrots and balls
of cotton… They willingly traded everything they
owned… They do not bear arms… With fifty men
we could subjugate them all… As much gold as you
need… as many slaves as you ask."

(Lights out on SAMMY *and* ANNIE.*)*

Scene 8

(The mushroom barn)

*(*BOB *pours pellet fuel substrate from five-gallon buckets into tall, plastic trash bags supported by cardboard boxes.)*

*(*TASHA *arrives in the doorway.)*

TASHA: Momma say take me ta school, say she feel sick.

BOB: What'samatter with 'r?

TASHA: Just sick, I dunno, I ain't the doctor.

BOB: You suppose ta been there two hours now.

TASHA: Well, I ain't.

BOB: I'm throwin' out the T V too, Tosh… no more
Britney, no more hussies, no more puberty boys. Your
teachers prolly too havin' them thoughts. I'm burnin'
every lil' overexposed piece you got. Then ya *haveta*
wear what we say cuz, well, cuz you won't have no
choice.

TASHA: Ya mean haveta wear what you say, momma
ain' care, she ain' even like lookin' my *face*, alone what
I *wear*, cuz I *remind* 'r too much. Now you gonna take
me ta school or I'm a haveta walk? Or ya want I should
put out my thumb?! I ain't care one way.

Scene 9

(A dive bar)

(SAMMY's on a stool at the bar.)

(The bartender is CLIFTON, *a Native-American, Lakota, 50's.)*

SAMMY: I wake up a booth sittin' a group a' U S Marines I ain't never met in a bar I ain't never been— "Excuse me", I slur, I say, "excuse me, SIR! —death before dishonor, SIR!—but where the fuck'm I at? Yeah I know it's a *BAR*, Jarhead, but where the fuck is the bar *LOCATED*?! ...*Tijuana*?! Well motherfuck an' goddamn, I'm so long a friggin' blackout I come to we at war with fuckin' Mexico. All I know's Flattop, we better the fuck win this one—y'all ain't win this one, I'm off ta Ireland, fish fer my supper... fer my *SUFFER*—piss my pants in goddamn peace, no judgements, no looky-loos, no johnny-laws neither... Judge not lest ye..." Lemme get two more, Clifton... Lila Itomni.

(CLIFTON tends to SAMMY's drinks as:)

(Lights rise on the interior of a car.)

(BOB drives. TASHA *is in the passenger seat.)*

(They don't look at one another, they don't speak.)

(Lights remain on SAMMY, CLIFTON, BOB and TASHA as lights rise on:)

(The kitchen:)

(SANDRA is doing the dishes and pots and pans from this morning's breakfast.)

(Lights remain on SANDRA in the kitchen and BOB and TASHA in the car as...)

(SAMMY *continues talking to* CLIFTON *in the bar—
throughout the above sequences—once* CLIFTON *has served
him his two drinks.)*

SAMMY: *(To* CLIFTON*)* This lil' fuck Flat-top with his
bigger flat-top leatherneck fucks aside him, he go "You
been out quite awhile, pally, welcome back, but now
you, uh…now maybe's time ya head back home."
Believe this prick? I bust'm open his fuckin' earhole
a bottle a' tequila, tellin' me what I should or should
not do. I hate mothafuckers tell me what I should
or shouldn't do. His buddies start *wailin'*, whoopin'
the shit outta me— "U S Marine Corps! U S M C!"
—they got blood pourin' out my goddamn forehead
inta my mouth, I'm curled up a lil' ball, tryin' juss…
tryin' keep my brains spillin' out—I hear a rib crack,
then another…then a, uh…whaja call, right here?
(Re: his shoulder)- hear that shit snap in half too—all
I see's black boots an' green camouflage, stompin',
kickin'—legs, boots, blood— "kick his ass, YA DRUNK
SUMBITCH!—teach'm a goddamn LESSON—
U S M C, U S A, U S A". I'm there tryin' ta enjoy
a goddamn drink! Thirty two years…trailer park-
flophouse-carseat-alleyways…never had no run-in no
goddamned Armed Force. Cross the frickin' border
first time come one/come all try an' get me. There's too
many goddamn Americans in Mexico—but ya never
see *that* shit in the news, do ya!? Ya never goddamn
hear about *that*! But not here, right? Not here with the
Indians. Ain't no need for no Canada, no Mexico, no
nothin'…no borders…no po-lice. Ain't no America
never gonna find us right here. Ain't that right, Cliff?
Ain't it right?

CLIFTON: You found it.

SAMMY: Wassat?

CLIFTON: You found it alright.

(Beat)

SAMMY: Seven shots! Seven shots, seven beers! *(Re: other customers)* Get these fellas whatever they want. They get it… They know *EXACKLY* what I'm talkin' 'bout. *(To the customers)* Lila itomni, boys. Nice ta see ya. *(To* CLIFTON*)* Lila itomni, friend. Good time by all. *(He drinks.)*

(Lights remain on SAMMY *as he drinks and smokes.*

*(*CLIFTON *pours seven shots and seven beers, lines them up in front of* SAMMY.*)*

(Lights remain on BOB *and* TASHA *in the car, silent, on the long drive to school.)*

(Lights remain on SANDRA… *now sitting at the kitchen table, smoking a cigarette.)*

(Lights remain on all as they rise on:)

(The classroom:)

ANNIE: *(Reading)* Spaniards "thought nothing of knifing and cutting slices off Indians to test the sharpness of their blades… and for fun beheaded them" too. Beheaded, class. That means to cut off their heads. *(She stops reading and closes the book. She looks at her young students. She speaks in her own words:)* We are peaceful in our hearts, class. In our souls. Each and every one of you. Greed and insecurities…and poverty and anger… and alcohol…these are *forced* upon us…by men who *suffer*…who possess deep jealousies…deep fears and anger. These are not who *YOU* are. These men are not your responsibility. You are each brave. You are each beautiful. You deserve *GOOD*. You *ARE* good. Say it with me, class: "I *AM* good. I *DESERVE* good". Say it: "I will be *HAPPY*". Say it with me, as one: "I will be *HAPPY*. I will be *LOVED*." "I will be *HAPPY*. I will be *LOVED*". Someone. *(Beat)* Please.

*(*BOB *puts the car in "park".)*

(SANDRA *snuffs out her cigarette.*)

(SAMMY *downs a shot.*)

(*Blackout*)

Scene 11

(*Studio apartment*)

(*Morning*)

(*Sun fights through slivers in the blinds.*)

(SAMMY *is on the floor.*)

(ANNIE *enters from the bathroom, dressed for work. She goes to the spiral notebook on the table, removes a sheet of paper on which he has written and puts it in the shoebox under the bed.*)

(*She nudges him with her foot. She leans down and shakes him a little:*)

ANNIE: Sam? Sammy, wake up. Sam.

(SAMMY *doesn't stir, doesn't wake.*)

(ANNIE *takes a whiskey bottle off the table, moves to the kitchen and fills it with water. She pours it over SAMMY's head, face, chest.*)

(SAMMY *stirs awake.*)

(ANNIE *leans down, kisses his forehead.*)

ANNIE: Have a good day.

SAMMY: Mmm.

ANNIE: Try to eat.

SAMMY: Mmm.

ANNIE: I love you. (*She exits.*)

(SAMMY *looks around. He reaches for his cigarettes. He gives up.*)

Scene 12

(Kitchen)

*(SANDRA, BOB and TASHA are finishing up breakfast.
TASHA draws. BOB reads* A Guide to Kansas
Mushrooms.*)*

BOB: *(Reading)* "Mushroom hunters who search Kansas
forests during the summer are often rewarded with
basketfuls of delectable Lactarius Hygrophoroides.
The orange brown cap and widely spaced gills, which
are well depicted in the photograph, make this species
easy to identify".

*(BOB tries to share the photo with an uninterested SANDRA,
who wheels off—exiting the room.)*

*(He tries to share it with an uninterested TASHA, absorbed
in her drawing.)*

BOB: Look. Tosh. Lookit the photo, please. I asked nice.

(TASHA quickly glances, then goes back to her drawing.)

BOB: That ain't lookin', that's bein' smart.

TASHA: Momma ain't looked.

BOB: I ain't talkin' 'bout momma, I'm talkin' bout me
an' you. You ain't never take no interest in things I
like. I look at your drawin's, don' I? I even hang some
on the walls. In the barn I got lots—an' right there on
the icebox. I take interest, you know I do. I do an' you
don't. How fair is that? *(Beat)* An' lil' reminder, Picasso,
these here mushrooms put goddamn food on the table.

TASHA: Duh, they *are* food.

BOB: I asked don't get smart. They also pay for those
drawin' pencils. An' that paper you drawin' on, an'
that orange juice, an' that lil' tank-top thing you got on
too. An' they pay for that make-up. An' that lipstick.

And for that, uh…whaddaya call…the soft blue over yer eyes?

TASHA: It's called eye shadow.

BOB: Well I don't like it. I ain't buyin' ya no more. It's too much. You're a little girl. No more make-up. *(Beat)* No more. *(Pause)* Come here. Come over here a second. I want you ta lookit these pictures with me.

TASHA: I ain't wanna.

BOB: I'll let you wear yer make-up ta school. I won't make you wash it off before ya go. *(Beat)* C'mere, Tosh. C'mon. Juss for a minute. *(Beat)* You can wear whatever you want.

(Beat)

(TASHA walks over. She stands next to BOB.)

(He shows her a picture and reads:)

BOB: *(Reading)* "Lactarius Indigo is a truly spectacular mushroom that is unfortunately rather rare in Kansas."

(SANDRA wheels back in, moving to the kitchen counter to fix herself another cup of coffee. BOB continues:)

BOB: "All parts of the fruiting body are silvery blue when young but gradually turn gray green with age. L-Indigo is a well known edible but tends to be grainy."

TASHA: Can I go back to my drawing now?

BOB: Yeah. Yeah, sure.

(TASHA returns to her drawing.)

SANDRA: One day, Bob. I'd like just one day…without hearin' 'bout your goddamn mushrooms. *(She exits.)*

(Pause)

TASHA: I dunno why you let'r talk ta you like that.

BOB: Eat your food.

TASHA: I ain't hungry.

BOB: Well drink your juice then. Draw. Mind your own business.

(TASHA *draws*. BOB *reads*.)

(Pause)

TASHA: I wouldn't let'r talk ta *me* like that.

BOB: She does talk ta you like that—she slaps ya cross the goddamn face, too.

TASHA: Yeah, but I'm not the one havin' sex with her.

BOB: I'll smack you clear cross this goddamn room, I will smack you. Lookit me...lookit me—I'll smack you right here.

(TASHA'*s temper explodes—she knocks her plate of food and orange juice across the table, spilling onto* BOB.)

TASHA: I'll kill you, I'll kill the both a' you and I can!! You ugly an' old an' fat an' she ain't even got no legs!! An' I'm pretty! I'm perfect! I'll kill you, I'll kill you both, I'll kill you, I'll kill you, I'll kill you...

(TASHA *is crying and pounding her fists against* BOB. *He restrains her. She calms a bit. His embrace becomes less forceful, more comforting, as she rests her head on his chest.*)

(*He puts his face to her hair. He kisses the top of her head. And once more*)

(*Suddenly, he forcefully pushes her onto the floor.*)

BOB: I'm sorry.

TASHA: I hate you.

BOB: I'm sorry.

TASHA: I hope you both die!! (*She runs out.*)

Scene 13

(The bar)

*(*SAMMY *and* ANNIE *are together at the bar.* CLIFTON *is behind it.)*

SAMMY: If I had a buffalo nickel for every brain cell rot gone I'd buy everyone here drinks til the day I die. People get fucked with one too many times? People don't fit in? These are *MY* people. Fuck anybody ever been in charge a' anyone else!! Another cranberry for my angel, Cliff, with a uh...with a splash a' soda, way she like.

ANNIE: *(To* CLIFTON*)* I'm okay, I'm still nursing this one.

SAMMY: Well this way you'll have back-up.

*(*SAMMY *gives* ANNIE *a quick kiss on the mouth.)*

ANNIE: I'm ready to go home, Sam.

SAMMY: *(To* CLIFTON, *re:* ANNIE*)* My greatest achievement right here, my big friend. *(Another quick kiss)* Reason not ta die in my sleep.

ANNIE: Sam...

*(...Another quick kiss—*ANNIE *tried to move away but it landed.)*

SAMMY: *(To the customers)* Eyes on yer drinks, men—thou shall not covet my perfection.

ANNIE: Sammy, please...

SAMMY: ...You wanna go, go. *(Beat)* Go on. You wanna go, go. *(Beat. Serenades her:)* There once was a lonely man on the lamb who roamed the land from land to land—but that man Sam he roams no more, no more. Whatta y'all havin' boys, who's drinkin' what? Clifton, cranberry-soda fer my better half.

ANNIE: I don't want one.

SAMMY: Why not?

ANNIE: I told you I wanna go home.

SAMMY: But I wanna stay. Me an' Clifton here, we uh…
we got things we need ta discuss a lil'. This a wise man,
here—he got wisdom. He got that, uh, Indian soul.
Ain't that right, Cliff? Tell'r I'm right.

CLIFTON: *(To* ANNIE*)* I'll get him home safe.

(Acknowledging CLIFTON*'s kindness:)*

SAMMY: Part prince, part Pope, part Pocahontas.

ANNIE: *(To* SAMMY*)* Tomorrow's the weekend. I don't
have school.

SAMMY: Saturday.

ANNIE: I'd like to spend the day together.

*(*SAMMY *tries to kiss* ANNIE, *she moves away.)*

ANNIE: I wanna do something nice.

SAMMY: Okay.

ANNIE: Something without you waking up feeling too
sick to do it.

SAMMY: I said okay. Whaddaya wanna do?

ANNIE: I don't wanna babysit and I don't wanna hear
you complain.

SAMMY: *(Gently)* Come here.

ANNIE: I'm serious, Sam.

SAMMY: I know.

ANNIE: I'm serious.

SAMMY: *(Gently)* C'mere.

ANNIE: No.

SAMMY: *(Sweetly)* C'mere. Come on. *(Beat)* C'mere.

(ANNIE *allows herself into* SAMMY's *arms. He gently kisses the top of her head as:*)

SAMMY: I'm gonna be home soon, okay? Clifton and me here we just…we got a few more things we need ta discuss. 'Bout…Mother Earth. Stuff like that. I love you, okay? Alright? I love you like ain't nobody never loved nobody before. Lookit me. Look. C'mere.

(ANNIE *looks into* SAMMY's *eyes. He playfully pinches her nose.*)

SAMMY: Whaddaya wanna do tomorrow? Mmph? You wanna go for a long hike? How bout horseback? Tha'd be fun, huh? Or maybe I make a nice breakfast in bed and…an' we just stay there all day? Mmph? Who's the luckiest man in the whole world, Annabelle? Go on, tell the truth—who's the luckiest man in the world?

ANNIE: You are.

SAMMY: That's right, me. I am. And who's the luckiest beautiful angel on earth? With the cutest lil' nose ta ever squeeze? Who would that lucky one be? (*A quick squeeze of the nose and kiss to her forehead:*) That would be you. (*To the bar*) THE GREATEST WOMAN EVER LIVED, MY PEOPLE—reason not ta take my last breath. (*To* ANNIE) I love ya, babe. (*To the bar*) I LOVE ANNABELLE STEVENSON—I LOVE HER!! Her choice in *MEN* is for shit, but…we do the best we can… I'll fight any man so much looks her sideways! Who wants what's what?! Bring it on, who wants what?!

ANNIE: (*Grabbing him*) Let's go, come on…

(SAMMY *breaks away violently:*)

SAMMY: Don't tell me what ta do or not do! You know I fuckin' hate that!

ANNIE: I know.

SAMMY: I hate it!

ANNIE: *(Gently)* Okay.

SAMMY: I fuckin' hate it.

ANNIE: Please.

(SAMMY gives her a quick kiss, then turns and addresses the others:)

SAMMY: Who's havin' what?! Cranberry, splash a' soda for my angel an' fill these men up, big Cliff, we got drinkin' ta do! *(He puts his hand over his mouth and does an "Indian war" chant, as a child would while playing Cowboys and Indians.)* Ay-ya-ya-ya-ya-ya-ya-ya-ya-ya… My People!

(ANNIE puts money on the bar and heads for the exit. CLIFTON joins her. SAMMY continues throughout:)

SAMMY: I had three broke ribs an' a broke in two fuck collarbone—them Marine cocksuck motherfucks!— "collarbone", that's it, my "clavicle"—more'n two hundred stitches cross my face, up my ear, inta my hairline an' out my ass.

(ANNIE exits. CLIFTON turns toward the bar. SAMMY continues addressing the others and the world:)

SAMMY: I hadda get the fuck outta there boys, too many 'Mericans down Mehico, boys, tried movin' up, get me ta Canada, can't stay stateside, can't go ta no jail—gotta run, keep movin', be a tornado…move-duck-bob-weave…*(War Cry)* Ay-ya-ya-ya-ya-ya-ya… Small town-small town, boxcar-boxcar, reservation-ta-reservation, BAM, straight between the fuckin' eyes, BAM, Annabelle Stevenson, arrow through the fuckin' heart, boys. Felt good for the first time in I ain't know how goddamn long. Felt right! Felt like a man suppose to. *(Raising a glass)* Ta every man got shot through the heart an' was happy that he did. Ta every man ever said "Fuck you Lonely Man, fuck you Angry Man, fuck you—get away from me—go on now, git, git away, you ain't welcome no-goddamn-more!"

CLIFTON: Sammy, c'mon...

SAMMY: ...Ta every warrior 'cided ta fight...

CLIFTON: ...Sam...

SAMMY: ...every warrior said "fuck you Wasichu, this ain't no cigar store an' I ain't no wooden!" *(War Cry)* Ay-ya-ya-ya-ya-ya-ya-ya...

CLIFTON: ...That's it, let's go, come on...

SAMMY: *(Chants/sings)* ..."I am roaming, Roaming, Restless, Aimless... On what road am I? The white man's road, Or the Indians?"...

CLIFTON: *(To the others)* ... He's alright, he's okay...

SAMMY: *(War cry)* ...Ay-ya-ya-ya-ya-ya-ya-ya-ya-ya...

CLIFTON: *(To the others)* I got'm—siddown—siddown, I got him! Sam! Sammy! SAM!!

(CLIFTON grabs SAMMY's arm. SAMMY breaks free:)

SAMMY: Nobody tells me what the fuck I'm s'pose ta do!!!

CLIFTON: It's time to go.

SAMMY: Nobody!!

CLIFTON: Let's get you outta here.

SAMMY: *(Sings)*
"One drunk Indian yells because he's mugged, Another complains his phone is bugged."

(CLIFTON grabs SAMMY again:)

CLIFTON: Knock it off, Sam—Stop, Sam...Knock it off!!!

(SAMMY struggles to get out of CLIFTON's two-armed bear hug, all the while singing to the others and the world:)

SAMMY: *(Sings)* "But nobody is getting hugged. Passerby say: 'How, Big Chief, What's your beef?' Ugh, Ugh, big chief, how, how. Hio, yana-yanay, hi-oh. Hear the po-lice whistle blow."

(SAMMY breaks free of CLIFTON and quickly punches him hard to the side of his head.)

SAMMY: *(Sings)* "Someone's pissin' in the snow, Tweet, tweet, ugh, ugh, clank, clank. Hio, yana-yanay, hi-oh." *(He stops singing. He looks around, at the others. He talks:)* "Got them, uh…them muscatel relocation blues. *(Beat)* Got them…long-haired…long-haired Injun blues."

(CLIFTON stares at SAMMY, who is now somewhat settled, somewhat conscious, somewhat free of his blacked-out rant. He looks to the others. He looks to CLIFTON.)

SAMMY: *(To CLIFTON)* Hey friend. *(He looks around for ANNIE, nowhere to be found.)* Annie? *(Beat)* Annabelle? *(He looks at the customers, his arms extended:)* My people!

Scene 14

(Mushroom barn)

(BOB is working with peroxide, agar, and petri dishes. The barn door opens, sunlight floods in.)

(SANDRA's in the doorway with a cane, wearing her prosthetics.)

SANDRA: I drove all over, I'm tired. I need you ta go, I've done my share— 'sides you're the one run her off anyway. *(She turns to exit:)*

BOB: Done your share a' what, Sandra? What've you done your share of?

SANDRA: Oh, fuck off, Bob, not now please with the big conversation.

BOB: That's yer answer ta everything— "Fuck off, Bob, fuck off" —well why don't you fuck off, how's that?

SANDRA: Fine, I'll fuck off while you find Tasha, I'm fuckin' off now, g'bye. *(She again tries to exit, but:)*

BOB: I ain't drank goin' almost two years, I ain't had no smokes goin' one-an-a-half—what the hell have you done?! One improvement?! You're her *mother*! There's only so much I can do!

SANDRA: I ain't asked you ta *DO nothin'* but go find her an' bring her home.

BOB: *LINDY* ain't comin' back, Sandra. The *TWIN* ain't comin', *HE* ain't comin', an' neither are your goddamn legs! Stop feelin' sorry for yourself an' start settin' an example!

SANDRA: I'm not the one locked in a room fulla manure all day...

BOB: ...It ain't manure...

SANDRA: ...Go find that girl. *(She exits.)*

BOB: *(Calling after)* I'm the one makin' money here, ain' I? Ain't I?! Buck-fifty a pound wholesale, wha'do you do?! Fuck the *MONEY*—who's makin' *breakfast*?! Who's takin' Tasha ta school?! Whaddayou do?! Mope mope, you ain't even *SLEEPIN'* with me goin' *TWO YEARS*! WHAT THE FUCK DO YOU DO?! SANDY?! You find her, Sandy! SANDY?! She ain't my kid! She ain't my goddamn kid!!

Scene 15

(Studio apartment)

(A dim bedside lamp is on. ANNIE *sits up. Waiting. Concerned. Silence)*

(Knock-knock-knock-knock)

CLIFTON: *(O S)* Annabelle. Annabelle, open up!

(Knock-knock-knock-knock-knock)

*(*ANNIE *turns on another light, puts on a t-shirt and sweats. All the while:)*

ANNIE: Just a second.

CLIFTON: *(O S)* Annie, open the door!

ANNIE: Coming.

CLIFTON: *(Knock-knock-knock)* It's Clifton. Annie?!

*(*ANNIE *opens the door. Draped over* CLIFTON's *shoulder is* SAMMY, *drenched in blood.)*

Scene 16

(The Kansas kitchen)

(In her wheelchair, no prosthetics, SANDRA *smokes in near darkness at the kitchen table.)*

(Long pause)

(Front door opens: it's BOB, *alone. He gives a slight shake of the head "no".)*

*(*SANDRA *snuffs out her cigarette and wheels herself to a nearby wall-mounted phone.)*

*(*BOB *sits at the kitchen table.* SANDRA *dials:)*

SANDRA: *(Into phone)* Hello? Hi, it's Sandra. I'm good thanks, how're you? That's good, that's…oh? Terrific, that's, that's real good, that's…congratulations…I will, yes. *(To* BOB*)* Sheriff Dave says hi. He an' Teri had a healthy baby boy. Eight pounds, nine ounces. *(Into phone)* He says congratulations and hi back. Yeah, it's, uh… It's Tosh again, run off…I know, yes, I…'bout thirteen-fourteen hours now. Sure, we will, we…yes… much obliged…I will…okay… Bye-now. *(She hangs up. She wheels off, exits.)*

*(*BOB *remains at the kitchen table.)*

(Lights remain on BOB *as…)*

(…Soft moonlight illuminates TASHA *sitting alone in a cornfield. She drinks from a bottle of blackberry brandy.)*

(Silence)

(Silence)

Scene 17

(Studio apartment)

*(*SAMMY *is on the bed, out cold/deep sleep. His bloody shirt has been removed. Some of his wounds have been bandaged, his blood wiped away.)*

*(*ANNIE *tends to him with a wet washcloth.)*

*(*CLIFTON *is across the room.)*

CLIFTON: You haveta get him out of here, Annie. Get him away from Little Eagle…outta South Dakota. Take him home, take him to rehab, take him to jail. They were gonna kill him if I wasn't there. They wanted to kill him and I don't know that I'll be able to stop them next time. I'm not sure I'd try. It's what he wants, he's just too much of a coward to do it himself. I'm sorry. But he needs to go home.

*(*ANNIE *opens a drawer in her bedside table. She finds what she's looking for: An old, small, leather bound book. From inside the book she retrieves a small, folded piece of paper.)*

ANNIE: He gave me a number the night he moved in. Could you watch him for me? Please? I need to use the payphone.

(ANNIE *exits.* CLIFTON *remains.*)

Scene 18

(*Kitchen*)

(BOB *is still seated at the table.*)

(*The phone rings.*)

BOB: (*Calling off*) Sandra?! SANDRA?! The phone!! (*He answers the phone.*) Hello? (*Beat*) This is Bob, who's this?

(BOB *listens to the voice on the other end as…* TASHA *enters through the front door carrying a bottle of blackberry brandy. She looks at him. He looks at her. She puts the bottle down and exits toward her bedroom.*)

BOB: (*Into phone*) Yeah. I'm here. (*He writes on a napkin as:*) Mmm-mm. Mmm-mm. Okay. Okay. (*He hangs up.*)

Scene 19

(*Studio apartment*)

(*A touch of moonlight creeps through the blinds.*)

(SAMMY *is asleep on the bed.* ANNIE *is in a chair beside him. He stirs awake. She comforts him. She wipes his mouth with the wet washcloth.*)

ANNIE: Hey.

SAMMY: Hey.

ANNIE: Hey.

(*Pause*)

SAMMY: I messed up again, din't I?

ANNIE: *(Meaning "yes")* Mmm-mm.

SAMMY: How come you think?

ANNIE: I dunno.

SAMMY: How come you think that is?

ANNIE: I don't know.

SAMMY: But you're still here, ain't ya? Always here. *(He tries to move and feels pain.)* Ow...uhh...

ANNIE: ...Sshh... *(Kisses forehead)* Go back to sleep. Get some rest.

SAMMY: Mmmm...

(Beat)

ANNIE: You finally made it to the bed, Sam.

SAMMY: Mmmm.

(Pause)

ANNIE: Goodnight.

(Pause)

SAMMY: I love you Annabelle Stevenson.

ANNIE: I love you Samuel McHenry.

(SAMMY closes his eyes.)

(ANNIE comforts.)

Scene 20

(The bedroom)

(SANDRA's on the bed.)

BOB: Roun' eleven-twelve hours total, seven-hundred miles. I need you an' Tosh ta come with. She's in her room, Sandra. She come home on her own, no one hadda find her, no one hadda drag her 'gainst her will. Bit a blackberry brandy, that's all. I'm askin' will you

come with? I'm goin' matter what. An' I want that you
both should come too. *Sandy?*

SANDRA: You want we go twelve hours cuz he needs
help?! Twelve hours?! I wouldn't help if he was
bleedin' up the goddamn drive.

BOB: Look, Hon…

SANDRA: …Don't "Hon" me, you sonuvabitch—he
killed my baby! He killed my baby girl, he took my
legs an' now we get a lil' phone call? He's in trouble?
He needs our frickin' *help*? They was only four years
old—Tasha cryin' in that back seat…Lindy lyin' dead
beside her. And I'm lookin' at him in his eyes…his
drunk bloodshot bullshit fuckin' eyes…beggin'…
"Help, Sam. Help your baby girl. Do somethin' for
somebody besides your own goddamn self!" An' he
open his door, Bob…he open his goddamn door…
barely but a scratch on him…and he run off. He just
run right off. An' now what? We get a phone call after
nine years? He got some new *girlfriend* say we gotta
come *save* him? Save'm 'fore what, he dies? I say go
'head, die.

BOB: I can't live in this house anymore.

SANDRA: There's the door.

BOB: Sandy, please, lookit me. Sandra, please…I'm
askin'…

(SANDRA *doesn't look.*)

BOB: I can feel in my bones what I feel…in my mind.
She needs her daddy, Sandy, she can't have me… she
can't…an' you don't need me neither…I'm gonna go
see'm, Sandy…he's my brother, he needs help…an'
I want the both a you ta come with. I'm gonna ask
he come back. He needs to be your husband again.
He needs to be Tosh's daddy. Lookit me. Sandy.

GODDAMN IT, LOOKIT ME!! LOOKIT ME!! LOOK
AT ME!!!

*(Bob grabs Sandra's head and twists her face so they make
eye contact.)*

(She spits in his face.)

(He takes a step back. Pause)

Bob: I'm leavin' first crack a' morn, seven hundred
miles. You comin' with or you gonna stay? Mmph?
Sandy? Should I wake you or should I not? Sandra, I'm
talkin' ta you. Are you gonna change yer mind or you
gonna stay? *Sandy?!*

Scene 21

(Studio apartment)

*(Annie has straightened up—the bed, trash, bottles,
ashtrays, etc. She is in the kitchen, putting the finishing
touches on assorted food items.)*

*(Sammy enters from the offstage bathroom. He wears
a button-up, tucked-in, short-sleeve, white shirt. And a
crooked, poorly-tied tie. Khaki cotton cargo pants. And fake
leather sandals.)*

*(His hair is wet and slicked-back. The blood has been washed
away, a lot of the swelling has subsided, but soreness
remains.)*

*(He hides his shaking hands in his pockets. This is the
longest he has been sober in a very long time. Not a drop
since last night.)*

(He stops. They look at each other.)

Annie: *(Affectionately)* Ohh…

Sammy: What?

Annie: You look handsome.

SAMMY: Yeah?

ANNIE: Yeah. You clean up real nice.

SAMMY: I need a drink.

ANNIE: You're doing great.

SAMMY: What time they suppose ta be here?

ANNIE: You'll be fine.

SAMMY: I don' know that I can do this.

ANNIE: And I know that you can. Come here. *(She goes to him and takes a closer look. As she unties and begins to re-tie his tie:)* You look real nice. Handsome.

SAMMY: I look okay for reals?

ANNIE: You look beautiful.

(Beat)

SAMMY: You think I look like I could be, um…a good father?

ANNIE: Absolutely.

SAMMY: Yeah?

ANNIE: A daddy any little girl would love to have. You just make sure she knows you love her just as much right back. *(Beat)* Do you like the tie I picked for you?

SAMMY: *(Meaning "yes")* Mmm-mm.

ANNIE: Do you like the shoes, the sandals?

SAMMY: Mmm-mm.

ANNIE: I used to get to tie my daddy's ties when his hands would shake too. I like ties. I think they make a man look real classy. My momma'd say, "Annabelle, there ain't nothin' classy about a man too drunk to tie his own tie." "He ain't drunk, Momma—he's hungover." There, let me see.

(ANNIE *stands beside him as they look in the mirror over the chest of drawers.*)

ANNIE: I told you. Real handsome. Like Brad Pitt.

(*Off* SAMMY's *disapproving look*)

ANNIE: He's from my home town. Don't worry, I like you more. (*She kisses his cheek.*) You're gonna do fine, okay?, I promise. Just be honest. Tell your daughter the truth. Tell them what you've told me.

SAMMY: What?

ANNIE: The things you said you've always wanted to. Okay? (*Beat*) Okay?

SAMMY: Yeah.

ANNIE: Promise?

SAMMY: Promise.

ANNIE: (*Staying with him, comforting*) Good. This is good, Sam. This is all good. You want something to eat, are you hungry?

SAMMY: Nah.

(SAMMY *loosens his tie a little. More shakes, sweats.* ANNIE *touches him, tries to settle him, knows he should eat.*)

ANNIE: (*Calmly*) I made your favorite—deviled eggs, two different kinds. And I got chips and salsa and cheese and crackers.

SAMMY: No, I…

ANNIE: (*Staying with him*) You want me to make you a sandwich? I got bologna, I got ham…

SAMMY: …WHAT IS THIS A FUCKIN' PARTY?! I SAID "NO"! (*Beat*) I'm sorry, I…I'm sorry. I gotta get outta here…

ANNIE: …Whaddayou mean?

SAMMY: *(Loosens tie a little more)* I gotta go, I can't breathe.

ANNIE: Have some water.

SAMMY: I DON'T WANT WATER!

ANNIE: Sam…

SAMMY: …I can't breathe, I need air, I can't breathe here…

ANNIE: …Sam, stop…

SAMMY: …My heart…

ANNIE: …Lie down…

SAMMY: …I can't, I…

ANNIE: …Stay here…

SAMMY: I said I can't!!

ANNIE: *(Grabbing him)* …You CAN!

SAMMY: *(Breaking free)* LET GO A' ME—LET GO!! *(Beat)* I can't breathe. *(Beat)* Okay?

ANNIE: Okay.

SAMMY: I need air. *(He unbuttons his shirt as:)* I needa get my head, walk around.

ANNIE: You need to stay sober.

SAMMY: I *AM* sober! *(He takes off his shirt and tie. He wears a tank-top underneath.)*

ANNIE: I said you need to *STAY* sober.

(SAMMY moves for the door:)

SAMMY: Ten minutes, I'll be right back.

ANNIE: Wait, I'm gonna go with you.

SAMMY: Ya can't, ya…ya need ta be here when they show up.

ANNIE: So should you. We have time, ten minutes like you said. Come on, let's go. What're you waiting for? *(Beat)* Why are looking at me like that? *(Beat)* Sam?

SAMMY: You look real pretty, Annabelle.

ANNIE: Thank you.

SAMMY: Thank you.

ANNIE: Where are you going? *(Beat)* Where are you gonna go?

SAMMY: You clean up real nice, too.

ANNIE: She's your daughter, Sam. She's your child.

(SAMMY quickly exits.)

ANNIE: Sam! *(She moves to the doorway, looks out.)* SAM!!

END OF ACT ONE

ACT TWO

Scene 1

(Studio apartment)

(TASHA is at the table drawing a replica of the Indian Chief painting. During the scene she also draws details of the apartment—furniture, the buffalo skin, etc.)

(ANNIE is standing, looking out the window.)

(BOB is sitting on the foot of the bed, eating from a plate of deviled eggs, chips, cheese, crackers, everything she had to offer.)

(Silence)

(BOB finishes his food.)

BOB: Mmm…very good. Thank you. *(He stands with the intention of bringing the plate to the kitchen.)*

ANNIE: Let me, please. Have a seat.

(ANNIE takes the plate. BOB remains on his feet.)

BOB: Much obliged.

ANNIE: Do you want more?

BOB: No thank you.

ANNIE: There's plenty.

BOB: I'm good. Thank you though.

ANNIE: I was expecting we'd be five.

BOB: Well, we only three, ain't we?

(An awkward moment. ANNIE *takes the empty glass out of* BOB's *hand as:)*

ANNIE: I'll refill your soda...he should be here any minute.

BOB: Any minute. *(He sits.)*

ANNIE: *(To* TASHA*)* Would you like more soda, sweetheart?

TASHA: Yes please.

*(*ANNIE *takes* TASHA's *empty glass.)*

ANNIE: *(Re: the drawing)* It looks just like him. You're very talented.

TASHA: Thank you.

ANNIE: You're welcome. *(She moves to the kitchen to deal with the ice and sodas as:)*

BOB: Oh yes, very talented, we're extremely proud of her. Never a problem, never a worry.

TASHA: Who's the man in the painting, Annie? Is that my father?

BOB: Your daddy ain't no Indian, girl, he's my brother.

TASHA: So?

BOB: So do I look like a goddamn Indian to you?

ANNIE: He's a very close friend of your father's. He's a Chief.

TASHA: *(To* BOB*)* You hear that? My daddy's friends with an Indian Chief!

BOB: Yeah, me too, we all went ta kindergarten together.

TASHA: Shut up.

BOB: You shut up.

*(*ANNIE *delivers* TASHA's *drink.)*

ANNIE: He's a famous Chief of the Lakota People.
Those are the Native Americans who live around here.
They're called Lakota.

BOB: You ain't Lakota.

ANNIE: No.

BOB: My brother ain't Lakota neither.

ANNIE: No.

BOB: And he ain't got no friends.

ANNIE: You don't know that.

BOB: No?

TASHA: *(To* BOB*)* You don't know anything about him!

ANNIE: Your daddy is a beautiful and special man.

BOB: That's why we drove twelve hours ta come see
him—to see his specialness with our own eyes.

ANNIE: *(To* TASHA*)* Speaking of eyes, I bet you saw a lot
of great things to draw out the car window, huh?

BOB: I ain't never seen a more sad-sack fucked-up place
my whole life. I wouldn't draw none of it, for what?
Ta hang on the bedroom wall so you could wake up
depressed in the mornin'? I wouldn't a even got out the
car if I wasn't so polite—I woulda stayed out parked
an' honked atchya. An' yet here you are, pretty young
thing—not Indian…and you decide this the place ta
pitch tent. Pretty girl like you. Maybe you ain't all
there. Maybe you two was made for each other.

ANNIE: Maybe. *(To* TASHA*)* I love your father very
much.

TASHA: So do I.

BOB: *(To* ANNIE*)* What the hell're you doin' here?

ANNIE: I came here to help.

BOB: Help who?

ANNIE: I'm a teacher.

BOB: Uh-oh—you're one a' those, huh?

ANNIE: I'm here for the same reason you didn't wanna get out of your car.

BOB: You're a "saver", huh? You "save"?

ANNIE: I'm a teacher.

BOB: Ya gonna save my brother? Mmph? How bout me? How bout Tasha? How many life jackets you got, sweetheart?

ANNIE: My name's Annie.

BOB: How many life jackets you got, sweetheart? *(Beat)* Mind if I smoke? Mmph?

ANNIE: No.

BOB: I'd done quit til up again this car ride, on account a' anxiety an' unhealthy thoughts. Tell me what the hell is he doin' here—why is he here?

ANNIE: Ask him.

BOB: He ain't here.

ANNIE: Ask him when he gets here.

BOB: I'll get a more honest answer outta you. We come all this way cuz you asked, not him. *(Beat)* He's my brother, ain't he? I wouldn't a come if I didn't care.

ANNIE: He was looking for someplace he wouldn't be judged.

BOB: Yeah? Meanin' what?

ANNIE: He thought maybe here, you know? With his, um... *(Aware of* TASHA*)* With his situation.

BOB: Ya mean him bein' a drunk?

ANNIE: He thought maybe here he'd be able to fit in.

BOB: An' does he?

ANNIE: No. *(Aware of* TASHA*)* I thought maybe you could take him back with you. And when the school year's over…I was thinking I could come join. I'll move to Kansas and we can get him the help he needs.

BOB: Yeah?

ANNIE: Yes.

BOB: What kinda help you think that is?

ANNIE: I'm not sure.

TASHA: *(Re: her drawing)* You wanna see it now, I'm all finished.

ANNIE: Wow, lookit that…it's beautiful.

BOB: Lotta talent.

ANNIE: It's really great, Tasha. I love this part, how the lines merge and the perspective gets…

BOB: …Oh for fucksake, where the fuck is he at? You don't have no phone, we can't call'm or nothin?

ANNIE: No, we don't here, but…

BOB: …Ya don't know where the fuck he is, ya ain't got no phone an' we're on the road all goddamn day cuz you're the one that fuckin' called *US*.

ANNIE: Please don't use that language.

BOB: What language would you prefer?

ANNIE: I don't think it's necessary.

BOB: Ya want I talk Injun instead? Bow-an'-arrow an' tomahawk, thass all I know…

ANNIE: …You shouldn't use profanity around children.

BOB: You even know a goddamn thing about my brother, huh? Or maybe ya just know the things he told you an' left the rest ta figger out in the dark? I could shed the light, if ya like.

ANNIE: Tasha, are you hungry yet?

TASHA: No thank you.

ANNIE: Are you sure, how about some more soda?

TASHA: Okay.

(ANNIE *takes her glass, goes to the kitchen, the fridge, etc, as:*)

BOB: Cuz he's opposite a' you, boy—look atchya… deviled eggs, "could I get you this?, you want more a' that?" My brother, well… he ain't like that. You save, he abandons. He run off his whole goddamn life, from he was a lil shit back ta the crib—back his sixth birthday—six years old momma an' daddy get that spoiled sumbitch a brand new Evel Knievel red-white-an'-blue bicycle, with ribbons an' a horn, an'… I never got no bicycle, never. An' he get a big ol' party ta go with—twenny, twenny-five kids, parents, couple teachers come too. Lil' spoiled Sam-Sam, I'm the *older* brother, I ain't never got shit. Not shit, but some late night visits and a bed in the barn while lil' spoiled Sam-Sam got his own goddamn room in the house with his own lock on the goddamn door. I'm sleepin' the barn one eye open, Sammy's Evel-fuckin'-Knievel with a ticket ta the rodeo. An' that spoiled-get-his-way-six-year-old-sonuvabitch—everybody singin' an' clappin' "happy birthday ta you, happy birthday ta Sam"… Sammy hop aboard his red-white-blue Evel Knievel, honk the horn an' ride off. "Bye, Sam, bye, Wow, lookit'm go—yippee!" An' then we all just sit 'round an' wait. An' wait some more. "When we gonna cut the cake?" "Shut up Bobby, we waitin' on Sam." "When we gonna pin the tail on the donkey?" "Shut up, Bobby, wait for Sam." "But when we gonna…Shut up Bobby, wait for Sam." But he's *SAM*, see? He don't care others care 'bout him cuz he ain't care 'bout others. An' the party gets dark, people get tired a' waitin'. They start sayin' their goodbyes. No more party an' still no Sam. Nobody left but mom, dad, and *ME* ta clean everything up. *(Beat)* Sammy come home three days later. Three days an' three nights. Said he was in a *cornfield*. Said he was *thinkin'*. Said he din't know no one was expectin' him to return to the party and he hopes we all had a good time. He was off *thinkin'*...about *life*, he said. Six years old. Thinkin' about his *own* life, ta be sure. *(Re:* TASHA*)* This one here the same goddamn way. No concern 'bout no one but theyselves.

TASHA: Juss cuz people don't care 'bout you don't mean they ain't care 'bout nobody!

BOB: I'll smack you right here, I don't give a shit where we at.

ANNIE: Stop it.

BOB: No, you stop! I ain't drive no twelve hours for a goddamn deviled egg! Where the fuck is my brother?!?!

ANNIE: I want you out of here right now—you can wait in the car, but you have to get out. Tasha, you can stay here.

BOB: Issat right?

ANNIE: Get out.

BOB: No thank you, I believe I'll stay.

ANNIE: I'm asking politely—please—will you *please* leave my apartment until he gets home?

BOB: I was hopin' ta order a pizza or chicken wings but seein' how ya got no phone, well, I guess I'll settle for a few more a' them eggs. Seein' as there's no phone... which means there's no way ta make no calls. And I'll take a refill a' soda please, too. *(He quickly finishes his drink and holds out his empty glass. Beat)* You're right, my apologies—no need ta wait hand-foot on a grown man.

(BOB *moves toward the kitchen.* ANNIE *steps aside to let him pass. She moves to the table, joining* TASHA. BOB *helps himself to deviled eggs, etc.)*

ANNIE: *(To* TASHA, *re: drawings)* Let me see.

(TASHA *shows* ANNIE.)

ANNIE: I don't know which one I like more. I like 'em both. There's no need for a competition, right, how's that sound?

TASHA: That sounds good.

BOB: I've decided to go back to Kansas alone and leave Tasha here with the two of you.

TASHA: *(To* ANNIE) Say "yes".

ANNIE: *(Beat)* I didn't tell you how much I loved your dress, did I?

TASHA: No.

ANNIE: I think it's real cute.

BOB: She don't like cute.

TASHA: Shut up.

BOB: She prefers ta look like a prostitute.

TASHA: Fuck you!

ANNIE: Hey...

BOB: ...I try ta tell'r, I say...

TASHA: ...Shut up!...

BOB: ...what's gonna happen she turn fourteen, fifteen...

ANNIE: ...You can't talk to her like that...

TASHA: ...I hate you, I hate you!...

ANNIE: ...Tasha, stop, ignore him, Tasha!...

BOB: ...Body parts poppin' outta nowhere, all them puberty boys lurkin' 'round...

TASHA: ...I hope you die, I hope you burn in hell!!! (*She runs out of the apartment.*)

BOB: An' there she goes.

(ANNIE *runs out [offstage] after her:*)

ANNIE: (*O S*) Tasha! TASHA!! TASHA!!!

(BOB *bites into a deviled egg. He sips his soda.*)

(ANNIE *re-enters, looking for her car keys as:*)

ANNIE: You can't talk to a young girl like that. You talk like that now, they never forget, she will never forget. She's your niece! (*Beat*) She rode off on a neighbor's bike.

(BOB *grabs the keys off the kitchen counter and gently tosses them underhand to* ANNIE.)

BOB: Shall we wait for her ta return before we pin the tail on the donkey?

ANNIE: Fuck you, my question is...

BOB: ...Fuck me?...

ANNIE: ...are you going after her or am I?...

BOB: ...[Fuck me]...

ANNIE: ...If I'm going I need to ask you to leave. Or you can go and I'll stay.

BOB: Why doncha send her father after her?

ANNIE: Are you going or am I?!

BOB: Maybe lil Sam-Sam ain't never comin' back at all—he certainly got the resume for it.

ANNIE: GET THE FUCK OUTTA MY APARTMENT!!

BOB: Sammy gets a bicycle, Sammy gets his own room, Sammy get ta have you too?...

ANNIE: ...Please...

BOB: ...that ain't fair, is it? You think that's fair?

ANNIE: I need to go find her.

BOB: Go find him too. Tell him no more— Tell'm I'm done with the hospitals an' the funerals an' the school drives an' the fucking everything! All these years— not knowin' he's dead, alive…he's with you… pretty young you. With your nice hair. Your nice eyes. Your nice legs.

ANNIE: Please. Step aside so I can go find her.*(Beat)* Please.

(Pause)

(BOB steps away. He turns his back.)

BOB: Go on. Keep cleanin' his mess. I'm done.

(ANNIE exits.)

Scene 2

(The bar)

(SAMMY is seated at the bar. No drink in front of him. CLIFTON is behind the bar.)

CLIFTON: I drank every day for thirty-one years. I haven't had a sip in the last five and a half.

SAMMY: Wow, they oughta put you on Mount Rushmore.

CLIFTON: "Put cork in bottle" one day at a time.

SAMMY: And take it back out every night.

CLIFTON: They wanted to carry you out to one of their trucks and drag you behind it.

SAMMY: Well they didn't.

CLIFTON: They were gonna kill you.

SAMMY: I didn't come for the wise elder shit, now gimme a goddamn drink.

CLIFTON: They were gonna tie your feet to the hitch, Sam...

SAMMY: ...Mmm-mm...

CLIFTON: ... And drag you through the Reservation.

SAMMY: Sounds painful.

CLIFTON: They wrote a sign to put around your neck, to parade the dead racist honky...

SAMMY: ...racist?...

CLIFTON: ...who doesn't know...

SAMMY: ...I ain't racist...

CLIFTON: ... when to keep his mouth shut...

SAMMY: ...How could I be racist?...

CLIFTON: ... A sign that read "I am not a warrior. I am a coward..."

SAMMY: ...coward?...

CLIFTON: ... "If found alive, kill me. If found dead, kill me again."

SAMMY: If I'm the coward why'm I the only one here, where they at?

CLIFTON: Go home, Sam.

SAMMY: I ain't see none a' them.

CLIFTON: Go home.

SAMMY: I am home!

CLIFTON: You're not even close.

SAMMY: I'm Irish!

CLIFTON: So?

SAMMY: I'm from rural Kansas, Sun City!

CLIFTON: Whaddoes that mean?

SAMMY: Keep shame outta sight, bury past with future, deny everything in between. Now gimme a goddamn drink.

CLIFTON: You pissed a lotta people off last night.

SAMMY: I was drunk.

CLIFTON: You piss a lotta people off a lotta the time.

SAMMY: Well I'm drunk a lotta the time, that's what happens.

CLIFTON: I saved your life.

SAMMY: Save yer own.

CLIFTON: I'm not gonna help next time.

SAMMY: There ain't no next time, no first, no last—all one, eternal, we got a understandin', me an' them.

CLIFTON: Go home.

SAMMY: We got a understanding, motherfucker!

CLIFTON: Get on 'The Red Road', Sam.

SAMMY: Fuck 'The Red Road'!

CLIFTON: Go home.

SAMMY: I DON'T WANNA GO HOME!

CLIFTON: Why not?

SAMMY: Stop tellin' me what I should or shouldn't do!!

CLIFTON: I asked why you don't wanna go home.

SAMMY: Cuz I don't feel like it, how's that?!

CLIFTON: Because why?

SAMMY: Cuz I wanna stay here!

CLIFTON: And you're gonna die here too.

SAMMY: Death's death.

CLIFTON: And what happens then?

SAMMY: Worms, maggots an' a high school marching band.

CLIFTON: And what about your little girl? She never gets to see her daddy again? What about your daughter, Sam?

SAMMY: What about her?

CLIFTON: You tell me.

SAMMY: I tell you?

CLIFTON: You tell me.

SAMMY: Whaddaya wanna know, am I deadbeat?—guilty—am I a asshole?—guilty—am I a lowlife scumsuck sonuvabitch?—throw away the fuckin' key, pal. Am I *COWARD* on top a' all that, too? Is that the question? Your lil' "accusation" with your lil' "friends" and their lil' "sign" tied tight 'round my white-boy neck? "Sammy The Little Coward White Boy?" Sure, why not, have at it—throw in coward too. I'm a coward, I'm a asshole, I'm a deadbeat, I'm a lowlife scumsuck sonuvabitch. And I'm thirsty! And I'm afraid. And I'm afraid I'll always be thirsty an' I'm thirsty I'll no longer be afraid an' blah-blah-bullshit-bullshit grow up an' get a fuckin' job!!

CLIFTON: Do you even know how old she is? There's a daughter out there wondering why her father hates her so much.

SAMMY: I don't hate her! I don't hate her at all. An' I reckon she goin' on 'bout twelve, 'leven now maybe, not sure. What? That make me a bad father? Mmmph!? Ya think so, that's what makes me a bad dad? Cuz I killed the other one!

CLIFTON: I know.

SAMMY: YOU AIN'T KNOW SHIT, YOU AIN'T KNOW A GODDAMN THING! SHE WAS FOUR YEARS

OLD! FOUR GODDAMN YEARS! Which makes her
what?, what's that make her, Cliff, the dead one? I
s'pose that makes her she ain't *NO* goddamn age *is she*?
She stopped ageing. Comin' home drunk from a friend
a theirs birthday -- their Momma was there, lotta other
parents there too. Not me though, I didn't make it, no. I
was at a bar. Time pass I go pick 'em up, get there safe
an' fine, alls I gotta do now's get 'em home same way.
Same twenny-five miles I drove drunk an' blacked-out
more'n two hundred, two thousand times. I wa'n't
bout ta give my wife the keys, though, no, I knew
best, of course, always did. Told'r "I'm fine, leave me
alone", told'r "Don't try to *control* me—tellin' me what
I should or should not do, I don't like that, blah-blah."
An' all I remember's after that's headlights comin'
face-on…an' me turnin' the wheel like this, this way, to
my left…bein' sure ta protect myself from the impact.
Bein' sure ta protect *my* side a' the car. An' then I run.
I din't stick around for my family, I din't stick 'round
try an' help nobody in no other car neither. I didn't
stick around. Hopped me a freight, never turned back.
An' you wanna know the best part? Huh? The best
part? When I was lookin' at my wife…with the whole
goddamn car crashed into her legs… my twin girls
behind me, one dead, the other pleadin' with her big
scared eyes… The best part, I thought, well…here's
your proof, Sam…here's what you was waitin' on…
your *CONFIRMATION*… You are a terrible human
being. Run, Sam—run. Now's your chance, before they
learn the truth about you. Hell, now's *THEIR* chance—
Go on. Let 'em be, Sammy. Go ruin someone else's life.
(Beat) Screw it, gimme a drink.

CLIFTON: That's it, screw it?

SAMMY: Why, ya think I'm wrong, mmmph? Ya think
she ain't better off without me?

CLIFTON: No.

SAMMY: Ya think I'm way outta line here, huh? Inside
a me's a goddamn superhero waitin' ta bust out if only
I CONCENTRATE an' FOCUS an' blah blah fuckin'
blah?! Mmmph? Tell me I'm wrong, go on—tell me
I'm the prize catch a' the century, I'm Superdad!, able
to kill babies in a single try. Maybe I shoulda took'r
with me, huh? Hopped the freight with'r in my arms,
plop her here top a' the fuckin' bar, order a Shirley
Temple— "what's that, sweetface? You don't want
Shirley Temple? You want what? Okay, well alright,
but just one—she'll have a Wild Turkey neat, Cliff, but
just one—she gotta drive'r drunk-ass Superdad back
home." Or I coulda stayed behind, done four-ta-six
in state pen an' then got out an' taken her ta the bars
back there. Cuz I would have! I would have, Cliff. I
know who I am. (Beat) So come on. Talk me out of it.
Tell me how misguided and lacking in wisdom I am.
Tell me how I woulda done different than I propose
an' woulda provided a nice, safe, happy life. I'm askin'.
Now's the time, Chief. Gimme some a' that good ol'
wise-man Indian shit. (Pause) I'm thirsty. May I please
have somethin' ta drink?

(CLIFTON reaches for a beer.)

SAMMY: Thank you. An' a shot a' bourbon too. An' a
shot a' tequila por favor.

CLIFTON: I won't save you again.

SAMMY: I know.

CLIFTON: You're on your own.

SAMMY: I know.

(CLIFTON pours the shots. SAMMY drinks.)

Scene 3

(Studio apartment)

(BOB is alone. In the kitchen. He puts out his cigarette. He eats some chips. He eats another deviled-egg.)

(He goes to the bed, soda in one hand, bowl of potato chips in the other.)

(He sits.)

(With the remote, he turns on the T V. Local news, talk of weather.)

(Pause)

(The front door opens. SAMMY enters.)

(BOB turns off the T V, stands, looks at SAMMY. SAMMY looks at him.)

(Pause)

BOB: They went lookin' for you.

(Pause)

SAMMY: Ya want a drink?

BOB: I'm alright.

(Beat)

SAMMY: No?

(Beat)

BOB: No.

(Pause)

SAMMY: Cuz ya gotta drive?

BOB: I quit.

(Pause)

(SAMMY goes to the kitchen. He stands on a chair and takes a hidden bottle out of a ceramic vase on top of the cabinet. He gets down from the chair and pours himself a drink.)

(He moves to the table and looks at TASHA'*s drawings.)*

SAMMY: Pretty good. Not bad.

*(*SAMMY *continues to look at* TASHA'*s drawings. He lights a cigarette. He offers one to* BOB.*)*

SAMMY: Smoke?

BOB: No.

SAMMY: Ya quit that too?

BOB: Got my own.

*(*SAMMY *continues looking at the drawings. Pause)*

SAMMY: How old she now? She eleven or twelve?

BOB: Thirteen.

SAMMY: Mmm.

BOB: Almost fourteen.

SAMMY: Mmm.

*(*BOB *lights a cigarette.)*

SAMMY: Really, these, uh…these drawin's…mmm… *(Beat)* Sandy come too?

BOB: [No].

SAMMY: Huh?

BOB: No.

(Pause)

SAMMY: You look alright. Better 'n I'd a 'spected, I suppose.

BOB: I wanna leave Tasha here with you.

SAMMY: Whaddaya mean?

BOB: Yeah.

SAMMY: What's that mean, wanna leave her?

BOB: I'm gonna leave her with you an' head back without her. Unless you wanna come with, then we can go all three.

SAMMY: I don't think so, no.

BOB: Which one?

SAMMY: Mmmph?

BOB: Which one you say "no" about? Leavin' her here or you comin' with?

SAMMY: I don't like neither one.

BOB: I can't be around them no more, Sam. I gave nine-odd years.

SAMMY: You're her Godfather, that's the oath you took.

BOB: In case anything happened to you.

SAMMY: Some'n did happen. Your job's ta take care an' see they alright—it don't have no nine-year expiration, that's for life.

BOB: It's been for life already.

SAMMY: No, it's been nine years.

BOB: My whole life's livin' 'bout you.

SAMMY: You took a oath, Bob, you know better.

BOB: Not so you could up an' run off, I didn't.

SAMMY: In case anything happened to my girls an' some'n happened! It's a promise for life ta take care, fuck you.

BOB: I need ta leave her here or I need you ta return. Are ya gonna return?

SAMMY: There's no time-limit on what occurred—I go back I'm put in state pen. Why in goddamn hell I'm a do some'n like that?

BOB: It was good ta see ya. Tell yer lady friend I said thanks. (*He moves toward the door.*)

SAMMY: Where you goin'? Hey—where the fuck
you goin'?! I CAN'T HAVE HER HERE WITH ME!
BOBBY?! I can't.

BOB: But she's yours.

SAMMY: I can't take care a' myself.

BOB: You gotchyer pretty lil girlfriend ta help.

SAMMY: This ain't no good here, Bobby. It ain't good.
(Beat) You always been more on your own feet, ya
know? I never seemed ta find me no solid ground,
quicksand. It's better with you. It's better.

BOB: *(Beat)* Did daddy ever take you out to the barn?

SAMMY: Whaddaya mean?

BOB: Did he ever take you out there with him?

SAMMY: I dunno.

BOB: No?

SAMMY: Not that I remember, I dunno.

BOB: For some father-son time? Just the two a' you?

SAMMY: No.

BOB: Sure?

SAMMY: Maybe ta feed somethin' or whatever, why?

BOB: *(Beat)* Where do they keep their retarded here,
Sammy? Here, in Indian Land?

SAMMY: I dunno.

BOB: How bout Kansas? Where do we keep the
retarded there?

SAMMY: In the basement.

BOB: An' do we let'm come out an' play from time ta
time?

SAMMY: No.

BOB: Or come up in the house on Thanksgiving?

SAMMY: I said "no".

BOB: How 'bout Christmas? Or Easter? We ever let'm come up an' eat, 'steada bringin' 'em food down in the dark?

SAMMY: No.

BOB: Never?

SAMMY: No.

BOB: *(Beat)* I better go, it's twelve hours. I don't wanna haveta pull over take a room.

SAMMY: You can't leave!

BOB: I get thoughts, Sam.

SAMMY: Whaddaya mean?

BOB: I get thoughts.

SAMMY: Everybody gets thoughts, so what, thoughts. C'mon buddy, have a drink with me, what's a lil' one gonna do ya?

BOB: I told you I quit.

SAMMY: Nobody goddamn drinks no more.

BOB: About Tasha.

SAMMY: What about her?

BOB: I gotta go.

SAMMY: You ain't got her in the basement, do ya?

BOB: No.

SAMMY: Somethin' with the accident got her messed in the head?

BOB: She's in your old room, Sam—the one with the lock on the door.

SAMMY: She ain't messed none from the accident?

BOB: No.

SAMMY: What about Sandra, she alright?

BOB: She's fine.

SAMMY: What about her legs?

BOB: They're beautiful.

SAMMY: Yeah?

BOB: Yeah.

SAMMY: Cuz they ain't look beautiful that night.

BOB: I live with them, Sam.

SAMMY: Who?

BOB: Sandra and Tasha.

SAMMY: That's good, yeah.

BOB: I've lived with 'em all nine years since that night.

SAMMY: Well, ya suppose to—ya took a oath.

BOB: Maybe a lil' different arrangement than you might 'speck. Sandra was in the hospital, Lindy was dead… mom an' pop gone. Someone hadda be there for Tasha. An' when Sandy got back, well… I just sorta stayed on.

SAMMY: Ya already said that.

BOB: You got everything an' got away with everything our whole life. You get three nights in a cornfield, I get three nights in the barn.

SAMMY: What're ya talkin' 'bout, cornfield?

BOB: I share a bed with your wife, Sam. In *your* bed, in *your* house…the house mom an' pop left *YOU* in the will, my *younger* brother got the goddamn house.

SAMMY: I was married with two kids. You still ain't over this bullshit? Hell, you been in nine years, you had more'n twice as long.

BOB: I fuck your wife, Sam! Every night I have relations with your horny beautiful wife! I fuck her, Sam. I fuck'r good, I fuck'r hard, and I fuck'r in your bed!

SAMMY: So?

BOB: So?

SAMMY: So what?

(The front door opens—it's ANNIE. *Followed by* TASHA.*)*

*(*TASHA *and* SAMMY *can't take their eyes off one another.)*

*(*ANNIE *closes the door.)*

(Long pause)

SAMMY: *(To* TASHA*)* Hello.

TASHA: Hi.

SAMMY: *(Beat)* Hi.

ANNIE: *(Beat)* Sam…this is…

TASHA: … I'm Tasha.

SAMMY: *(Beat)* I know.

*(*BOB *sits on the foot of the bed. He lights a cigarette.)*

SAMMY: Come here. Lemme get a better look atchya.

*(*TASHA *runs into* SAMMY's *arms.)*

SAMMY: Whoa, whoa… There ya go, that's it…that's it.

*(*TASHA *holds him with all her might.* SAMMY *struggles to reciprocate. He can't. Not fully)*

(He breaks the embrace.)

SAMMY: Okay. That's enough. *(Re: a drawing)* I like this, you're…you're a good draw-er.

TASHA: It's of your friend.

SAMMY: Who?

ANNIE: *(Continuing the lie)* Your friend, Sam. The important Lakota Chief who I told Tasha you were friends with.

SAMMY: Yeah, he... *(Points to the painting)* That's him right there, ain't it?

TASHA: What's his name?

SAMMY: His name, oh...His name?

ANNIE: Clifton.

TASHA: Clifton?

SAMMY: Yeah, that's right... Chief Clifton. That's a mighty pretty dress ya got on.

BOB: I bought it for her.

SAMMY: *(To TASHA)* It's pretty, it's...

BOB: ...When's the last time you bought'r anything?

SAMMY: I like it. It's got a lotta flowers on it.

TASHA: I wore it special for you.

BOB: Kickin' an' clawin'.

TASHA: Don't listen to him.

SAMMY: I'm not. An' I'm glad you wore it special for me. Thank you. You're a pretty girl, ain't you? You got the cutest lil' nose that ever did squeeze. *(He pinches her nose. He can no longer fight his tears. He begins to shake and sweat.)*

TASHA: What's wrong?

SAMMY: You got so big.

TASHA: I don't remember.

SAMMY: It's been a long time.

TASHA: You're sweating.

SAMMY: Yeah.

TASHA: And shaking. Are you okay?

SAMMY: Yeah, I'm…some'n I ate, maybe, I'm alright.

TASHA: I don't like when I get sick.

SAMMY: No…I don't like when I do neither.

(Regarding one of his tattoos:)

TASHA: It says "Lindy".

SAMMY: What?

TASHA: On your arm. Right there, it says "Lindy".

SAMMY: Yeah, it…yeah.

TASHA: That was my sister.

SAMMY: Yes. And this one right here's for your momma: "Til I Die S W" *(He shows her a tattoo on his stomach.)*

TASHA: What's that mean, "S W"?

SAMMY: Sandra Wilkinson. That was your momma's name before mine.

BOB: That's her name again now, she changed it back.

SAMMY: *(To* TASHA*)* Boy, I juss…just ta look atchya.

TASHA: What?

SAMMY: It's nice to see you.

TASHA: It's nice to see you too.

SAMMY: Real nice. All tall an'…pretty dress an' everything…pretty girl.

TASHA: Thank you.

SAMMY: You're welcome. Yeah. Wow.

TASHA: What?

SAMMY: Nah, just…nothin'. Just wow. *(Beat)* Now come on, c'mere…gimme 'nother hug real quick 'fore you gotta get goin', ya got a long haul ahead a' ya.

TASHA: Whaddaya mean?

SAMMY: We had a nice visit.

TASHA: I wanna stay with you.

SAMMY: Well...

TASHA: ...Please?...

ANNIE: ...Or maybe you could go with them, Sam?

SAMMY: Mmmph?

ANNIE: You could go with them if you like.

TASHA: You could come back home, daddy.

ANNIE: Would you like that, Sam? You could go with the two of them and then I can come join when school's out.

SAMMY: I can't, I...

ANNIE: ...Sure you could. Go with them, Sam—I'll catch up real soon, the school year's almost over.

SAMMY: I think maybe, um...

ANNIE: ...It's only six weeks. You can go home, and get settled, relax a little away from the bar...

SAMMY: *(To* TASHA*)* ... I know, I got a real good idea! Me an' Annie, we can come together, after the school year, ya see?, the two of us...

ANNIE: ...Sam?

SAMMY: ...Cuz she got these uh, you know, commitments an' responsibilities she gotta tend to, she got these Indian school kids, see?, and they *depend* on her, so...but when she's done with the... *(To* ANNIE*)* That's a great idea, baby. That's a...that's the best idea I heard in a long damn time. *(To* TASHA*)* Six weeks, hell, that ain't nothin', is it? Not compared ta what we been through, right? Six weeks ain't nothin'!

TASHA: Nah, that ain't nothin'!

SAMMY: Nothin'!

TASHA: Nothin'!

BOB: Alright, let's go.

TASHA: NO!!!

SAMMY: You're a little fighter and you ain't never give up for no thing or nobody. Okay? Say okay.

TASHA: Okay.

SAMMY: Say "daddy I promise".

TASHA: Daddy I promise.

SAMMY: I promise you too.

TASHA: You promise you'll come see me in six weeks?

SAMMY: Stick a needle in my eye.

TASHA: How come you got momma an' Lindy tattoos but not one with my name?

SAMMY: No, I do, I…I got more'n that, than a tattoo, I…

TASHA: …But why come you didn't get a tattoo of me?

ANNIE: Sam, we almost forgot, remember? You asked me to tuck it away so you could give it as a surprise, remember? Look how beautiful it is. *(She has removed a cheap beaded necklace from her bedside drawer.)*

ANNIE: Here, I'll give it to her.

(ANNIE hands it to TASHA.)

TASHA: *(To SAMMY)* You got me a necklace?

SAMMY: Not just any necklace, no, but, um, some'n better, somethin'… Much better than any dumb tattoo. This is uh, this is a very very special necklace. This necklace, it—it's been blessed, yeah… It was blessed by a real life Lakota Chief.

TASHA: By Chief Clifton?

SAMMY: Right, that's right, yeah, by him right there on the wall, Chief Clifton—I went to'm, see, I made a

special visit—this mornin' in fact, when I knew you
was on your way an'...I told'm, I said... Hello Chief!
...Chief Clifton, my buddy... I have me one very
special visitor comin' all the way here ta see me today.
The *most special* visitor in all the whole vast world.
My daughter, Tasha. That's right, Chief Clifton, my
daughter is comin' to see her old man! An' I want a red
carpet an' a hot air balloon an' a thirty-five gun salute.
I wanna climb up inta the heavens an' pull down a big
bright star an' pin it right there on her chest! I wanna
do somethin' *real nice*, important like she is, like she
deserve, real nice. And Chief Clifton said he could do
more than a air balloon, more than a star ta pin on yer
chest—and he give me that necklace—and he bless it
with over ten thousand years a' history—he bless it
with uh...with strength, and uh... With the strength
of a *WARRIOR*. Not a coward, you unnerstand? But of
a warrior on "The Red Road"—who will be strong...
strong against anything and anyone. Stronger than a
Fightin' Irish. Strong as a Indian Chief.

TASHA: And what else?

SAMMY: What else?

TASHA: What else did he bless it with?

SAMMY: Yeah, with uh...with *HAPPINESS*, too, that's
right, with uh... With a happiness you'll always have,
an'...can take with you wherever ya go...

TASHA: And what else? Daddy, what else?

ANNIE: And what else, Sam? Tell her what he blessed it
with most of all.

SAMMY: And um...most of all, he uh... He blessed it
with *love*. Most outta everything else, so...so you'll
always know how much you're loved. Okay? Alright?
Say "alright".

TASHA: Alright.

SAMMY: Alright, good. Good. *(Beat)* C'mon, let's try it on.

(SAMMY helps TASHA slip the necklace over her head and around her neck.)

SAMMY: Perfect.

(TASHA looks at herself in the mirror.)

TASHA: Perfect.

(Beat)

BOB: You could still come with us, Sam…if ya want?

ANNIE: I'll catch up in six weeks.

TASHA: Six weeks ain't nothin'! Say it daddy. Come home.

(They wait for SAMMY's response:)

SAMMY: I need ta stay here for a little while, I… *(To ANNIE)* I'll go with you, when school's out. *(To TASHA)* That's right—nothin', six weeks! Not compared ta we been through. Come here. Give yer daddy a…gimme a nice ol' big one. Say goodbye.

(TASHA hugs SAMMY. She intends on never letting go. He can't reciprocate.)

(He breaks the embrace, but continues to hold her arms.)

(He has trouble making eye contact. He wants to say something, but no words come.)

(He moves to the duffle bag filled with pots and pans. He picks it up.)

SAMMY: This is good too.

ANNIE: Sam…

SAMMY: You can hit on it whenever ya get real pissed off. Whenever ya wanna hurt somebody or hurt yourself.

(SAMMY *drops the bag at* TASHA's *feet, walks away, enters the offstage bathroom and closes the door.*)

BOB: C'mon, let's go. Come on.

(TASHA *runs to the bathroom door and puts her ear up against it.*)

BOB: Get away from there. We're goin' home, let's go.

(TASHA *remains.*)

BOB: I said let's go. Step away.

(TASHA *moves away from the door.*)

(*Pause*)

BOB: (*To* ANNIE) Anyway… (*Pause. Then to* TASHA:) Say goodbye, Tosh.

ANNIE: I'll see you soon, okay? Take your drawings.

(TASHA *goes to* ANNIE *and gives her a hug. They separate.*)

TASHA: Could you tell him I left the drawings for him?

ANNIE: Yes.

TASHA: And could you tell him I love him more than anything in the world?

ANNIE: You tell him. Go on.

BOB: Go on, just hurry the fuck up.

ANNIE: (*To* BOB) I want you to shut up! (*Beat. Then to* TASHA) Go on. (*Beat*) Go on. Take all the time you want.

(TASHA *goes to the bathroom door. She listens, her ear against it.*)

TASHA: Daddy? Daddy, can you hear me? I love you. Thank you for my necklace. Thank you for everything. I'll see you in only six weeks, okay?! Okay? (*Pause*) I love you more than any dad in the whole world.

(*No response*)

(TASHA *turns, walks over and grabs the duffle bag and heads for the front door.*)

(*She stops.*)

TASHA: I'm glad my daddy met you. Goodbye.

(BOB *holds the door for* TASHA *as she exits.*)

(*He exits and closes the door.*)

(ANNIE *moves to the window. She looks out. She waves.*)

(SAMMY *exits the bathroom as* ANNIE *continues looking out the window.*)

(*He has a bottle in his hand. Pause*)

(*She continues looking out the window.*)

SAMMY: You okay? Mmmph? (*Beat*) I don't really think I deserve you, do I? You prolly waitin' on someone I ain't never gonna be.

(*Still with her back to him:*)

ANNIE: (*Quietly*) [You're probably right.]

SAMMY: Huh? (*Beat*) What was that?

(ANNIE *turns to face* SAMMY.)

ANNIE: I said you're probably right.

(*Beat*)

SAMMY: Is this that day? Huh? Is that what this is? That day I knew, but you denied or lied to yourself about? Lied ta *me*? Huh? Issat what this is? Is this the goodbye day?! Confirmation day? Is this that day, Annabelle? IS THIS THAT FUCKIN' DAY?!?! TELL ME, ANNABELLE! TELL ME! IS IT FINALLY THAT FUCKIN' DAY?!

ANNIE: Yes.

SAMMY: What? (*Beat*) Wha'd you just say? (*Beat*) Say it again. What'd you just say?

ANNIE: I said yes, Sam. It's finally that fucking day.
(She exits.)

Scene 4

(Cheap motel room)

(BOB is sitting at a small table. He talks on the room phone. TASHA is not in the room.)

BOB: *(Into phone)* I took a room. *(Beat)* Eyes got too tired, hardly keep 'em on the road. *(Beat)* Sometime early, guess, get a good start. *(Beat)* Mm-mm. *(Beat)* No. *(Beat)* Alright then. 'Nite.

(As BOB hangs up, lights remain on him as…)

(…a light illuminates SANDRA in the kitchen, near the phone on the wall.)

(She hangs up the phone. She lights a cigarette.)

(He lights a cigarette in the motel room.)

(Silence)

(Lights remain on SANDRA and BOB as…)

(Dim, soft, light rises on…)

(Studio apartment as ANNIE enters.)

(Stuff is broken, the T V is on, bottles are strewn about. SAMMY is passed-out on the floor.)

(ANNIE turns off the T V.)

(She gets undressed. She gets into bed.)

(She turns out the light.)

(Lights go out on the studio and kitchen [ANNIE, SANDRA, SAMMY] but remain on BOB in the motel room as…)

Scene 5

(Cheap motel room)

(Simultaneously as lights go out on ANNIE/SANDRA/
SAMMY...*)*

*(...*TASHA *emerges from the bathroom, talking, picking up
where she obviously left off.)*

*(*BOB *remains seated at the small table, smoking.)*

TASHA: An' when he comes I'm gonna take him ta
meet all my friends, an' to the pond ta dive off the cliffs
tagether, an' we gonna spend all kindsa time an' do all
kindsa fun things—he was better than I ever thought
he coulda—he was so nice an' so handsome—I can't
hardly believe you two's brothers—and he got Indian
friends—you ain't have no Indian friends—you got the
T V and mushrooms—and his girlfriend, I think she
real pretty, an' nice—an' I think she in love with him
cuz the way she look at him, an' she ain't talk ta him
like momma talk ta you or nuthin', she talk real nice.
An' my necklace, look how beautiful. Look.

*(*BOB *doesn't look.)*

TASHA: Blessed by a real life Indian Chief named Chief
Clifton! An' when my daddy come visit in six weeks
I'm gonna keep him all ta myself an' there ain't nuthin'
you or momma or nobody can do about it. He gonna
sleep in my room an' we gonna lock the door so when
y'all wanna try ta get in on our time ya can't cuz we
won't open cuz we got nine years a' catchin' up an' we
gonna take our time—cuz I love him—an' he love me—
an' from now on wherever he go I go too. And I wanna
thank you for that. I wanna *thank you* for bringing me
with you. I want you should know that, cuz... well,
cuz...today was the best day ever happened in my life.
(She takes off her dress, gets under the covers) G'nite. Don't

let them roaches bite. *(She turns off her bedside lamp, lies down, closes her eyes.)*

(Pause)

*(*BOB *looks over.)*

(Pause)

(He looks away. He puts out his cigarette. He takes off his shoes and pants. He sits on the foot of his bed in his boxers and t-shirt and socks.)

(He looks toward TASHA *once again.)*

(Silence)

(Silence)

(He stands. Looks at her. Walks over to her bed. He stands over her. She doesn't stir.)

(Lights shift as he moves into her bed.)

T*(he reality and tone of the world change as he remains in the bed as she lifts her head...)*

(Simultaneously...)

(Lights rise on SAMMY, *on the studio apartment floor, as he lifts his head and looks over to* TASHA, *who is looking at him—through walls, across state lines, inside each others' desperate, helpless thoughts.)*

(Lights rise and remain on SANDRA, *still in the kitchen.)*

*(*TASHA *and* SAMMY'*s eyes remain locked. Their eyes reach out to one another, but their bodies and mouths remain helpless, still, silent.)*

(Lights slowly fade to black on SANDRA.)*

(Then also slowly fade to black on SAMMY—*as his head drops slowly to the floor and his eyes close...)*

(...while TASHA'*s eyes close and her head goes back to the pillow...)*

(..and BOB *sits up, his back to her...)*

(…as the lights become "real" again.)

(Pause)

(He moves to his own bed, on top of the covers. On his back, eyes on the ceiling.)

(Silence)

(He turns off his bedside lamp.)

(Blackout)

Scene 6

(Studio apartment)

(Morning. A gloomy, cloudy sky provides a dim light that struggles to pierce the blinds.)

(SAMMY is still on the ground.)

(ANNIE wakes.)

(She puts on a pot of coffee.)

(She looks at SAMMY. She notices something different this morning.)

(She moves toward him. She nudges him with her foot. No response. Another nudge.)

ANNIE: Sam? *(Another nudge, a little harder.)* Sammy? Sammy, wake up. *(She leans down. She turns him over to see his face. She shakes him and slaps him:)* Sammy. Sammy, no—Sammy wake up—wake up—Sam—Sam, no—SAMMY?! No no no Sam-no no… Sammy, please, please, Sam, SAMMY!!! WAKE UP!!!!

Scene 7

(Kitchen)

(SANDRA smokes at the kitchen table.)

(Silence)

(The front door opens. TASHA enters, carrying the duffle bag of pots and pans. The necklace is around her neck.)

SANDRA: Hey.

(TASHA ignores SANDRA and exits toward her room.)

SANDRA: Tasha, wait…Tosh? I need to talk to you.

(No response)

(BOB enters and shuts the door.)

BOB: Hey.

SANDRA: Hey.

(Beat)

BOB: I got work ta do in the barn.

SANDRA: Sam's girlfriend called. A little while ago.

BOB: Wha'd she want? *(Beat)* She ain't got nothin' on you.

SANDRA: Sam's dead, Bob. He died sometime this morning.

(Beat)

BOB: Well. *(Beat)* We tried. *(Beat)* Can't no one deny us that. *(Beat)* I don' think we need ta tell Tosh. I don't see any reason ta make her upset.

SANDRA: She ain't your daughter, she's mine.

(Beat)

BOB: Alright. *(Beat)* I'll be in the barn.

(BOB exits.)

Scene 8

(Studio apartment)

(CLIFTON and ANNIE sit in silence.)

(Not looking at one another)

(On the table, between them, is the shoebox full of SAMMY's letters. A few of the letters are out of the box, on the table.)

(Neither of them touch or read the letters. They just sit there. Together. In silence)

Scene 9

(TASHA's room)

(The duffle bag of pots and pans hangs from the ceiling.)

(TASHA hits it. She hits it again. She hits it again. Again. Again…)

(SANDRA enters without knocking. She is in her wheelchair, without her prosthetics. She has an Express Mail package in her lap.)

(TASHA stops hitting the bag.)

SANDRA: It's from Annie. It's for you.

(TASHA takes the package. She sits on the bed. She opens it.)

(It's the shoebox full of letters.)

(She opens the shoebox. She sifts through the many sheets of paper.)

(She tries to read. She doesn't know how.)

(She offers the top page to SANDRA.)

(SANDRA takes the page. As she reads she does her best to not cry in front of her daughter.)

SANDRA: *(Reading)* If your reading this right now it means I never woke back up. My heart beats real fast

when I try ta sleep like I feel its gonna just stop or
maybe even explode. Either way I know I'm gonna die
as soon as I'm suppose ta start ta dream instead. It aint
nobodies fault or nothin like that. Its just my heart got
too much. I can feel it in my wrists right now beatin'
with my fingers bout maybe two hundred beats in one
minute. But I want you to know Tasha that my life and
my death are my own and there aint nothin anyone
including you coulda done to stop that. You and your
sister Lindy were my two angels and your mother
when we first met and decided to fall in love she was
my miracle on this earth. Please I want you to be sure
to tell her that for me. And that she was so beautiful.
That's true she was one of the most beautiful people
you ever saw on the inside and out. I'm sorry I run
out on you Tasha. And that's not your fault or your
mommas fault or nobody else's neither. I just didn't
know how to stay. I love you so much you make my
heart beat more than two hundred beats in one minute.
Like its tryin to beat outside my body and run away
to go and be with you in your body and enter to the
inside of your heart and then they can join together
as one big giant heart. Can you feel it inside you right
now when you read this? Cuz that's where I bet it is.
Okay I'm tired now its time for me to shut my eyes.
Give your mother a kiss. Try to be a good daughter
for her and not too much trouble. And don't drink no
alcohol cuz you probly born some way you don't know
about it til its too late. Ya gotta stay on "The Red Road"
Tasha. That's what my Indian friends call it when you
don't drink no alcohol. Bein on the red road. Its a long
road and its got a lotta blood on it but ya gotta promise
me you gonna least try. I'm lookin down on you right
now and I'm smilin' cuz your sisters here beside me
and we both lookin down on you and on your momma
and we both say hi and send love. And your sister
wants you to know shes okay and not to worry. And

I'm okay too so don't worry bout me neither. I love you
Tasha. Your Daddy. Sam.

(SANDRA *puts the note back in the box. She turns her*
wheelchair around and wheels out.)

(TASHA *looks at the notes. One after another. She then*
begins to put them back in the shoebox.)

(River of Sorrow *by Antony and the Johnsons begins*
to play, and continues as, one at a time, the following are
revealed and continue simultaneously:)

(Studio)

(ANNIE *is packing a suitcase, throwing out bottles, trash,*
etc.)

(Mushroom barn)

(BOB *is sitting. Looking around. Deep in memory*)

(Bedroom)

(SANDRA, *in her wheelchair, without her prosthetics, stares*
at her reflection in the mirror. She unbuttons her blouse.)

(TASHA's *bedroom*)

(*She has finished putting the letters in the shoebox. She*
removes the pots and pans from the duffle bag and replaces
them with clothes and the shoebox full of letters.)

(Studio)

(ANNIE *stops packing. Starts unpacking. She stops. Looks*
around. She grabs her teacher's bag and school books and
exits.)

(Bedroom)

*(*SANDRA, *in front of the mirror, removes her blouse. She gently runs her fingers along her breasts.)*

(Mushroom barn)

*(*BOB *stands. Looks around. Exits)*

(The bar)

*(*CLIFTON *pours a round of beers.)*

(Classroom)

*(*ANNIE *enters. She looks around. She puts her bag on the desk. She remains on her feet.)*

*(*TASHA*'s bedroom.)*

(She exits—the duffle bag draped over her shoulder, the beaded necklace around her neck.)

(Bedroom)

*(*BOB *enters. He approaches* SANDRA. *She doesn't see him at first.)*

(He leans down. He kisses her neck. She resists. He continues. She acquiesces.)

(Classroom)

*(*ANNIE *sits at her desk. She begins working on the day's lesson plan.)*

(Mushroom barn)

(TASHA enters, the duffle bag over her shoulder. A can of gasoline in her hand. She slowly, deliberately pours gasoline over everything in the barn.)

(Bar)

(CLIFTON pours a round of shots.)

(Bedroom)

(BOB kneels before SANDRA and begins to gently kiss her legs at their points of amputation. She cries. He comforts. He kisses. She allows him to continue.)

(The barn)

(TASHA lights a match. She hesitates.)

(Bedroom)

(BOB's kisses move from SANDRA's legs to her mouth. She kisses him back.)

(Barn)

(TASHA throws the match into the middle of the barn.)

(A fire erupts.)

(She stares, watches the fire grow.)

(The barn is engulfed by flames.)

(The whole world seems to be engulfed and everyone in it— CLIFTON, ANNIE, BOB, SANDRA, even TASHA—disappears in its light.)

(But then TASHA emerges, walking, leaving her home behind—a lone figure illuminated by the light of the flames.)

(The duffle bag is over her shoulder.)
(The necklace is around her neck.)
(A long red road stretches in front of her.)
(She stops.)
(She stares ahead.)
(Blackout/silence)

END OF PLAY

www.ingramcontent.com/pod-product-compliance
Lightning Source LLC
Chambersburg PA
CBHW052207090426
42741CB00010B/2447